TYRONE POWER

A One-Person Play in Two Acts
By

Michael B. Druxman

The Hollywood Legends

TIME & PLACE

ACT I

1958: A hotel room in Madrid, Spain.

ACT II

Later that day.

SETTING

The play is set in the living room of a luxury hotel suite in Madrid, Spain.

Entrance to the room is UR, with sliding glass doors to a balcony DL. Entrance to the bedroom and bath are UL.

Furnishings include a sofa, armchair, desk with phone, coffee and side tables. A wet bar is UC.

TYRONE POWER

ACT I

AT RISE: TYRONE POWER, *44,
enters from the bedroom; goes to
the bar and pours himself a drink.
Bearded, he is dressed in a sport
coat, slacks and wears an open shirt.*

After a moment, the PHONE RINGS.

TYRONE POWER
(*Answers phone*)

Hello?

Hi!

We got in okay.

Deborah's out with one of her friends…

Seeing a little of Madrid.

And, I'm just taking it easy today.

When do we start filming my scenes?

That'll let me adjust to the time change.

You're surprised I did this one?

—

I'm surprised I did this one.

I thought I was done with swordplay.

It was a two-picture deal…

And, the money they offered…

I couldn't pass up.

I get a percentage of the gross on both pictures.

But, after these two, I'm going to take a rest.

Maybe lay off for a year or so.

Spend time with Deborah and the new baby.

He…

I hope it's a "He"…

He's due in late January.

That sounds good.

Dinner tomorrow or the next day.

Talk to you later.

> *He hangs up; downs his drink.*
> *Becomes aware of the audience.*

Hello.

You've been listening.

I'm going to be a father again.

I have two daughters.

It will be nice to have a son.

Tyrone Power, Jr.

I know…

Not a very original name…

But, we have to carry on the tradition.

The name goes back to my great grandfather…

Also Tyrone Power.

He was an Irish actor and comedian.

Died in 1841.
                    (*Chuckles*)
Before I was born.

There's a lot of distinguished people…

Distant relatives…

…In my background.

Evelyn Waugh, the writer…

Even Laurence Olivier…

But, you're here to hear about me…not them.

I'm thinking of writing my autobiography…

And, I thought I'd bounce the highlights off you first.

Previews of coming attractions.
                              (*Beat*)
My father was, also, "Tyrone Power".

His friends called him "Fred".

Actually, there were several "Tyrone Powers" in our
family"

Tyrone Power Senior…

Tyrone Power, The Younger…

Even I get them mixed up.

My mother was also a Shakespearian actress.

I was born in Cincinnati, Ohio.

Tyrone Edmond Power, Jr.

Also known as: Tyrone Power III.

I know. It gets confusing.

I was rather a frail, sickly child…

So, my parents moved to Southern California.

And, they divorced…

My father wasn't the most faithful husband.
                    (*Beat*)
Mother took my sister, Anne, and me back to Cincinnati.

Went to school there.

Worked part-time as a soda jerk…

A theater usher at the Orpheum Theater in Cincinnati.

And, I didn't see my father for many years.

But, we exchanged letters.

There was never any question that I would go into the theatre.

Mother saw to it that I had lessons in diction…voice control.

Then, when I was sixteen…

Father returned.

———

It was a good reunion.

He gave me advice on how to be a Shakespearian actor.

Took me to Chicago where he was doing *The Merchant of Venice.*

Got me a small part.
(Beat)
One night…the actor playing "Shylock"…

He missed his mark and, accidentally, stuck a large knife into the scenery next to my head.

You can imagine how shaken I was.

"You're not hurt boy," my father whispered. *"Keep on playing".*

"Keep on playing."

Invaluable advice.

I did other small roles with my father.

Even on radio.

And then, we went to Hollywood.

I joined him on the set of a movie he was making.

The Miracle Man.

—

It was a remake of the old Lon Chaney silent film.

Sylvia Sidney was in it…Chester Morris….

One day on the set…

My father had a heart attack.

He died in my arms.

We had just reunited…

Been working together…

He was only 62.

After a long moment:

My father may have had a famous name in the business…

That didn't help me.

I didn't have any practical acting experience.

Sure, I did bits in plays…a couple of pictures.

Flirtation Walk with Dick Powell and Ruby Keeler.

Look quick. You might even spot me.

But, nobody in the film business was willing to take a chance and give me a *real* role.

I was young…determined…

Penniless…

Lived in an attic…

My diet was stolen milk…

And the avocados growing in the landlord's garden.

So, what did I do?

I went to New York.

Maybe somebody would give me a chance there.

And, you know who did?

Katharine Cornell.

She cast me in her production of *Romeo and Juliet.*

No, I wasn't "Romeo".

That was Maurice Evans.

Orson Welles was "Mercutio".

And, I was "Benvolio".
(In character:)

"Part, fools!

14

"Put up your swords; you know not what you do."
                              (*As himself:*)
That was my breakout role.

I was approached by a talent scout from Universal
Pictures.

He offered me a contract.

I didn't know what to do.

I asked Miss Cornell.

She advised me to turn down the offer.

She felt I should have more experience before I was
tied down to a studio.

I took her advice.

Turned the contract down.

Later, I was in Cornell's production of *St. Joan.*

Got sixty dollars a week for that one.

And, that's when a talent scout at Fox spotted me.

He gave me a screen test.

Sent it to Darryl Zanuck in Hollywood.

He didn't like it.

Said I looked like a monkey.
                    (*Chuckles*)
Back then, my hairline was low…

And, I had thick bushy eyebrows,

They were a continuous straight line above my nose.

Thankfully, Zanuck's wife, Virginia, was in the
screening room that day.

She convinced her husband that I had "something".

That my eyebrows could be shaved…

And my hairline raised.

They shot another test.

Signed me to a contract.

After they disposed of my simian features…

My first film was *Girl's Dormitory*.

I had one line.

I went up to Simone Simon, and said:
                    (*In character:*)
"*Could I have this dance?*"

That was it.

Would you believe that, at the film's sneak preview….

Most of the comments talked about the good-looking fellow in the final scene?

I guess Zanuck figured he had something in me.

After another picture, he cast me over Don Ameche in *Lloyds of London*.

Madeleine Carroll was the leading lady.

And my friend, George Sanders…

Who I'll be dueling with in this new picture…

Was the heavy.

Lloyds of London was a major film.

An epic!

Yes, it was semi-fictional…

But, it did deal with the start of Lloyd's insurance business…

The Battle of Trafalgar….

The movie was a hit.

 And, over night…

At twenty-one…

I was a star.

People were comparing me to M.G.M.'s Robert Taylor….

Warner Bros.' Errol Flynn.

Zanuck gave me a raise.

Starred me in more films.

Several with Loretta Young.

Love Is News…

George Sanders was, also, in that one.

Café Metropole…

Second Honeymoon…

And then, I did *In Old Chicago*.

That's one you remember, right?

In 1936, M.G.M. had made *San Francisco* with Clark Gable.

That picture recreated the 1906 great earthquake.

Two years later, Zanuck tried to borrow both Gable and Jean Harlow for *In Old Chicago*…

He was going to re-stage the 1871 Chicago fire.

Louis B. Mayer turned him down.

So, Zanuck cast me and Alice Faye and Don Ameche in the picture.

He was going to out-do Metro.

That twenty-minute fire sequence cost $150,000 to stage.

It burned for three days on the Fox back lot.

In Old Chicago got an Oscar nomination for Best Picture.

And, Alice Brady *won* the Supporting Actress Award.

I don't know why *she* should win.

She played "Mrs. O'Leary"

It was her cow that started the fire.
                    (*Chuckles*)
The original idea for *Alexander's Ragtime Band* was that it was going to be a biography of Irving Berlin.

After all, it was his music.

But, Irving didn't like that plan, so they just fictionalized the plot and used his songs.

"The International Rag"…

"Blue Skies"…

"When the Midnight Choo-Choo Leaves for Alabam'"…

"Alexander's Ragtime Band"…

Lots of others.

Alice Faye was in it.

Don Ameche…

And, Ethel Merman.

This was the first time that Berlin had worked with Merman.

He was so impressed with her that he wound up writing *two* Broadway shows for her:

Annie Get Your Gun and *Call Me Madam.*

I don't know why Berlin never wrote a musical for me.

Just because I can't sing.
                    (*Chuckles*)

After *Alexander*…

Zanuck made a big mistake.

He loaned me to M.G.M. in exchange for Spencer Tracy.

Fox wanted him for *Stanley and Livingston*.

Metro wanted me for *Marie Antoinette* with Norma Shearer.

What can I say about *Marie Antoinette*?

It was an expensive film.

It got several Oscar nominations…but didn't win any.

And, quite simply:

I was not shown to the best advantage.

In fact, after he saw the film, Zanuck swore he would never loan me out again.

I had offers to do *Golden Boy* at Columbia.

King's Row at Warner Bros.

But, Zanuck said "*No!*"
                    (*Beat*)
In all fairness, he did make it up to me.

He gave me a choice …

Within reason…

…of my scripts and co-stars.

He even let me use his private steam room.

I was the only actor who had that privilege.

So, what was the first picture I did after *Marie Antoinette*?

Suez.

I built the canal…

With help.

And, I also met Annabella.

She was my French co-star.

Did I fall!

It didn't matter that she was four years older than me.

We went out to dinner a few times.

She was married…separated…

But, once she got her divorce…

We got married in 1939.

I even adopted her daughter, Anne.

Zanuck wasn't too happy with our union.

Being married would hurt my box-office.

He even offered Annabella a lucrative film deal back in Europe.

She turned him down…

And, the son-of-a-bitch suspended her.

I should have told him where to go.

Gone on strike.

I couldn't.

Zanuck had me by the short-hairs.

When Annabella and I went to buy a house…

I found out that I was broke.

Turns out that my trusted business manager had been stealing from me for years.

I'm an actor. I don't know anything about money.

Annabella bought the house…

And, I had to smile and go back to work at Fox.

Zanuck did put me in some good pictures.

I did my first film in Technicolor.

My first Western.

Jesse James.

We shot that in and around Pineville, Missouri.

That was Jesse James' territory.
                    (*Sings*)
"*Jesse James was a lad that killed many a man,
He robbed the Glendale train…*"

Who says I can't sing?

*But that dirty little coward
That shot Mr. Howard
Has laid poor Jesse in his grave.*

I was Jesse James.

Henry Fonda was Frank James.

And, John Carradine played Bob Ford.

He was the dirty little coward who shot me in the
back…

While I was hanging a picture.

(*Chuckles*)
At the premiere, some young boy kicked John in the shin.

John's a damn good actor though.
(*Beat*)
While we were in Missouri…

I had a fling with a local girl.

I guess that's one of the advantages of being a movie star.

Except, in this instance, she got pregnant.

Had a son.

Put him up for adoption.

I didn't know that the boy even existed until afterwards.

Spent a small fortune searching for him.

No success.

I want a son.
(*Beat*)
Selznick was considering me for the part of "Ashley Wilkes" in *Gone with the Wind*.

That didn't happen.

Not sure if Zanuck killed it or not.

Maybe I wasn't the perfect Southern gentlemen…

But Leslie Howard was an Englishman.

Instead, I did *Rose of Washington Square* with Alice Faye and Al Jolson.

It was a "fictionalized" telling of Fanny Bryce's story.

(*Chuckles*)

Fictionalized?

The film even included Bryce's song, "*My Man*".

My character was based on her husband, Nicky Arnstein, who went to jail for fraud.

Bryce sued Fox…and the case was, eventually settled out of court.

(*Beat*)

In *The Rains Came*, I had tinted skin.

Played a surgeon from India.

Myrna Loy was in it…George Brent…

It was adapted from the Louis Bromfield novel.

Not my favorite movie.

I got the first "Harvard Lampoon" Worst Actor
Award for my performance.

And then, I went to Europe…briefly

With the threat of war, we had to get Annabella's
parents to America.
(*Lights cigarette*)
I did *Brigham Young-Frontiersman*.

Dean Jagger was "Brigham Young".

I may have had first billing, but I was just one of his
followers.

After that, I did *The Mark of Zorro*.

"Zorro" is Spanish for "fox".

I dueled with Basil Rathbone.

He was the heavy.

And, an excellent fencer…unlike me.

I had to be doubled in the fancier parts.

Basil is such a nice man

He had dueled with Errol Flynn in films like *The
Adventures of Robin Hood*.

Somebody asked him how I compared to Flynn when it came to swordplay.

He said: *"Tyrone Power is the most agile man with a sword I've ever faced before the camera.*

"He could have fenced Errol Flynn in a cocked hat."
(*Beat*)
We're lucky we didn't get arrested doing that picture.

Linda Darnell played my love interest.

And, she was only sixteen at the time.

Linda and I did another picture together:

Blood and Sand.

John Carradine was also in that one.

And, it was Rita Hayworth's first Technicolor film.

It was about bullfighting.

To prepare for the role, Annabella and I attended a real bullfight.

Big mistake!

We sat in the V.I.P. seats right in front.

Watching that…slaughter…

I became violently ill.

They had to take me out of the arena.

Not too good for my heroic image is it?
                    (*After a moment; Chuckles*)
Blood and Sand gave Fox some censorship issues.

Remember, this was a 1941 movie.

And, both Anthony Quinn and I are…

Let's just say that a bullfighting outfit did not hide
our masculinity.

Neither of us had anything to be ashamed about.

Yet, adjustments in our costumes had to be made….

Which made them rather uncomfortable to wear.
                    (*Beat*)
I did *A Yank in the R.A.F* with Betty Grable….

Son of Fury with Gene Tierney…and George
Sanders.

Played a bastard in that one.

Not personality…by birth.

The Black Swan was pirate movie.

Maureen O'Hara…

—

George Sanders…

He had a scruffy beard in that one.
                    (*Beat*)
My marriage to Annabella was not going well.

I wanted a son…and she wasn't giving me one.

To be honest…

Both of us were unfaithful to the other.

She was having an affair with some wanna-be writer…

And, I got involved with Judy Garland.

Yes, *that* Judy Garland.

She wanted me to leave Annabella for her…

But, that didn't happen.

I guess I was trying to save my marriage.
                    (*Beat*)
Then, came Pearl Harbor.

I was a young man…in good health.

I was expected to join the military.

Which I did.

—

Enlisted in the Marine Corps.

But, before I went on active duty, I was allowed to finish the patriotic picture I was making.

It was a submarine picture.

Crash Dive.

Could you think of a better recruiting film?

In the movie, I'm credited as "Tyrone Power, U.S.M.C.R."

After boot camp, I attended Officer's Candidate School.

Became a second lieutenant.

I was already an experienced amateur pilot.

Had 180 solo hours before enlisting.

With a little more training, they made me a first lieutenant.

I was a good student.

They wouldn't let me fly combat missions.

Said I was too old.

I've always wondered if Zanuck had something to do with that.

I piloted cargo planes.

North Carolina…

California…

Later…

Probably when Zanuck wasn't paying attention…

I got to go to the Marshall Islands.

Carried cargo in and wounded soldier out during the battles of Iwo Jima…

Okinawa…

Got several medals for my service…including two bronze stars.

I was released from active duty in January of 1946.

I've stayed in the reserves ever since.

I'm a major now.
(Beat)
Zanuck was so happy to see me home…

He not only gave me a new contract that only required me to do two pictures a year for Fox…

32

He, also, gave me a present.

A surplus DC-3.

I call it "The Geek".

Why "The Geek"?

You'll understand in a bit.

I take it up as often as I can.

But, not when I'm making a movie.
                    (*Beat*)
Zanuck may have been delighted that I was home.

But, my wife wasn't.

She went back East to do a Broadway play.

Sartre's *No Exit*.

She played a lesbian.

While she was there, she also announced that we were legally separated.

"Incompatibility of careers."
                    (*Beat*)
The first picture I did after I got back was *The Razor's Edge*.

I played "Larry Darrell".

It was a much meatier role than anything I'd done before the war.

Adapted from the Somerset Maugham novel.

Gene Tierney was in it…

John Payne…

Clifton Webb…

Herbert Marshall played Somerset Maugham.

And, Anne Baxter won a Best Supporting Actress Oscar.

(*Chuckles*)

I fell in love with Gene Tierney.

She was still married to Oleg Cassini, the dress designer.

They were separated.

We went out.

Rumors began to circulate that we were a couple.

At the film's premiere, I even gave her a scarf with the word "*Love*" embroidered on it.

And then, she told me that she was seeing somebody:

John F. Kennedy.

He was the son of Joseph Kennedy.

Had more money than God.

And, he was, also, interested in politics.

So, I backed off.
(Beat)
Edmund Goulding was the director of *The Razor's Edge*.

He was the best I've ever worked for.

One day, he had a rather strange request of me.

To capture the essence of my character, he didn't want me to have sex until after certain scenes…

The ones with the Yogi in the East…

Had been filmed.

I'm a good soldier.

I agreed.

I'd done my research.

I knew that…

In nothing are the wise men of India more dead right…

———

35

Than in their contention that…

Chastity intensely enhances the power of the spirit.

Later, I found out that Goulding asked this of all his leading men.

It was his way of achieving a certain look.
                    (*Chuckles*)
I couldn't stop laughing.

I had some introspective lines in *The Razor's Edge*.
                    (*In character:*)
"I don't think I'll ever find peace until I make up my mind about things…

"You keep asking yourself what life is all about.

"Is there any meaning…or is it just a stupid blunder?"

Makes you think, doesn't it?
                    (*Beat*)
I was thirty-two when I did *The Razor's Edge*.

Ten years older than "Larry Darrell".

And, I looked it.

The Razor's Edge was such a success that…

At my request…

Fox agreed to cast me in *Nightmare Alley*.

My favorite of all my films.

Definitely not a typical Tyrone Power role.

Yes, it was a "dark" film.

I wanted to change my image.

I couldn't be a swashbuckler all my life.

Zanuck tried to talk me out of it.

But after *The Razor's Edge*…

I guess he wanted to keep me happy.

They paid fifty thousand for the rights to the novel.

And they went all out.

The studio built a full carnival set on the back lot.

They hired carnival workers…

Sideshow attractions.

Joan Blondell was in the picture…Coleen Gray…

I played the "Geek".

Actually, *I wound up* as the "Geek".

I'm not talking about my plane.

Though that's how it got its name.

A "geek" is a fool or simpleton.

It's a term used in carnivals and circuses to describe the "wild man".

A typical geek show in the last century would have a person on stage biting the head off an animal…

And, drinking its blood.

I know…

Even more disgusting than a bull fight.

Zanuck cut a lot of those scenes.

He, also, ordered a new ending be shot.

He didn't want the picture to be such a downer.

Didn't make any difference.

The film got excellent reviews…

I thought I might even get an Oscar nomination.

I didn't!

Nightmare Alley flopped at the box-office.

Zanuck didn't publicize it.

And, he pulled it from release after a few weeks.

He knew that audiences weren't going to accept me in that sort of role.
>   (*Beat*)
Before my next picture, I went on vacation.

Cesar Romero and I went to South America for six weeks.
>   (*Suddenly Irked*)
There have been these "stories" about me and Cesar.

Also, stories about me and other people:

George Cukor, the director…

Clifton Webb…

Van Johnson…

Even Cary Grant…

All gossip!

Gossip doesn't make the stories true.

Cesar and I went to South America for one reason.

We were going to do a picture set there.

Captain from Castile.

I know we wound up shooting it in Mexico, but…

After a moment:

Forget it!

You're going to believe what you're going to believe.

That's what makes good copy.

> *He pours himself a drink.*
> *Downs it, then pours another.*

Let's take a break.

Later, maybe I'll tell you about Lana.

And, that's true.

> *He does the drink.*
>
> *LIGHTS FADE.*

END OF ACT ONE

ACT II

AT RISE: *It's later that same day. Power, dressed as before, sits in the armchair, reading his script.*

After a moment, he becomes aware of the audience.

TYRONE POWER

You're back.

I'm sorry if I was abrupt before.

Sometimes I hit on memories that can be…
uncomfortable.

But, if I'm thinking on writing my autobiography…

I guess I have to deal with them, don't I?

Why am I in Madrid?

We're doing a Biblical picture.

Solomon and Sheba.

I'm "Solomon"…

Gina Lollobrigida is "Sheba"…

———

41

And, once again, George Sanders is my nemeses.

It's another swords and sandals picture…

But, with King Vigor directing, it should be a good one.

King also directed *Captain from Castile.*

"Butch" played Cortez…

"Butch"?

That was my nickname for Cesar Romero.

I played a dashing Spaniard who joined Cortez in the conquest of Mexico.

All 140 minutes of it

I know. It may have been a long movie…

But, it made money.

And, we even had a live volcano erupt in the picture.
(Beat)
It was around that time that I met Linda Christian.

Annabella was, finally, a closed chapter.

The divorce did cost me a small fortune.
(Beat)
Actually, I was dating Lana Turner when I met Linda.

Linda was doing a small role in *Green Dolphin Street* at M.G.M.

Lana Turner was the star of that picture…

Lana and I were "involved" at that time.

There were plenty of pictures of us in the fan magazines.

The relationship didn't end well.

Louis B. Mayer was not about to let one of his biggest stars have a child out of wedlock.

We were not about to get married…

After that, Lana and I…

After a moment:

Linda Christian was born in Mexico…

The daughter of a Dutch petroleum engineer.

She spoke seven languages.

A sometimes actress.

Once she was involved with Errol Flynn.

And her real name wasn't "Linda Christian" …

Even I have trouble pronouncing what it really was.

We married in January of 1949…in Rome.

They called it "The Wedding of the Century".

We had two daughters, Romina and Taryn.

But, she lost a couple of babies along the way.

Both sons.

She really wanted an acting career.

And, she blamed me when I wouldn't push for her to be in one of my films.

I wanted a wife and mother to our children…

Not an actress.

And now, we're divorced.

But, we'll deal with that later.
                    (*Beat*)
After *Captain from Castile*, I did *The Luck of the Irish*.

I played a newspaperman in that one…

Cecil Kellaway played a leprechaun.

And, *he* got an Oscar nomination.

I guess that's why they called it *The Luck of the Irish*.

I did *That Wonderful Urge* with Anne Baxter.

That was really a remake of *Love Is News*…

The movie I'd made with Loretta Young.

Zanuck was running out of original scripts, and he was re-working the studio's old scripts.

After that, he cast me in *Prince of Foxes* with Orson Welles.

Welles did it because he was shooting his production of *Othello*…and he'd run out of money.

We shot the picture in Italy…

With all those palaces and beautiful scenery…

In black-and-white.

Zanuck was trying to save money.

Can you believe that?

We shoot a costume picture in Italy in black-and-white!

After that, I did another costume picture with Welles.

He was still trying to finish *Othello*.

The Black Rose.

That one was shot in England and Morocco.

I played a disinherited Saxon nobleman.

And, this one *was* in Technicolor.

> *After a moment:*

After *The Black Rose*, I took a break from filmmaking.

I went to England and starred in the London production of *Mister Roberts*.

Jackie Cooper played "Ensign Pulver".

This was the first stage play I'd done in nine years.

Played it for six months.
> *(Ironic chuckle)*
As much as I enjoyed doing it…

While I was away, Zanuck, apparently, was not missing me.

Gregory Peck was the new top leading man at Fox.

Close behind him were Richard Widmark and Victor Mature.

When I returned to Fox…

I was cast in *American Guerrilla in the Philippines*…

I didn't want to make that picture.

Neither did Fritz Lang, the director.

We both had bills to pay.

After that, I did a western.

Rawhide with Susan Hayward.

It was an okay script…

But, Gregory Peck got *The Gunfighter*.

And, that's "a classic".

Why couldn't I get "a classic"?
                    (*Beat*)
I guess that Zanuck still wanted to keep me happy…

So, some of the next few pictures I did were shot in in Technicolor.

After *I'll Never Forget You*…

That was a remake of a 1933 Leslie Howard picture, *Berkeley Square*.

Had to do with time travel.

Ann Blyth was in it…

And, it bombed at the box-office.

People were watching television then.

We were competing with "*The Lone Ranger*" and "*Dragnet*".

Pony Soldier was in color.

But, no "classic".

I played a member of the Canadian North West Mounted Police.

Even though we shot that in Arizona.

After that…

Zanuck loaned me out.

I guess he didn't have anything for me.

Once again, since I only had a few films left on my Fox contract, he wanted to keep me happy.

I went over to Universal and did *The Mississippi Gambler*.

I guess Rock Hudson or Jeff Chandler weren't available.

But, Piper Laurie was in it…

———

Also, Julie Andrews.

This was my first film away from Fox since *Marie Antoinette*.

I even had a profit share on that one.

Made over a million dollars.

I'm sure Zanuck was delighted about that.
(*Chuckles*)
In fact, later "*Lux Radio Theater*" broadcast a sixty-minute adaptation with me.

After *The Mississippi Gambler*, I went back on the stage.

Producer Paul Gregory offered me *John Brown's Body*:

A dramatic reading of Stephen Vincent Benet's epic Civil War poem.

"John Brown's body lies a-mouldering in the grave."

The moment Gregory suggested that I participate, there was nothing further to discuss.

I even turned down the Burt Lancaster role in *From Here to Eternity* to do this one.

Who knew?

Charles Laughton was directing *John Brown's Body*.

Judith Anderson, Raymond Massey and I performed in formal dress on an almost empty stage…along with a chorus.

We did a sixty-city, twenty-eight state tour.

And, we recorded it for Columbia Records.

After the tour, I went back to Fox.

Did *King of the Khyber Rifles*.

I know…

It was no *John Brown's Body*.

It was a remake of an old Victor McLaglen movie, *The Black Watch*.

Once again, Zanuck was remaking his old movies.

If you already own the film rights to a property, you don't have to buy them again.

This one was set in India…

But, we shot it in California.

It's cheaper to create India than to send a whole cast and crew there.

I was really a bit old for the part…

Certainly a bit old for my leading lady: Terry Moore.

And, can you really see me as a British officer?

After a moment:

In October of 1954, Linda and I announced that our marriage had ended.

"Career incompatibility".

That seems to be a common reason for Hollywood divorces.

Linda said I was "cool and distant".

And, of course, I didn't get her parts in my movies.

That divorce cost me a million dollars.
(*Beat*)
I missed out on *The Robe*.

Richard Burton did that one.

Marlon Brando got *Viva Zapata*…

I'd been off the screen for a couple years.

But, when I made my return, it was one of the best roles I ever had.

———

And, it was for Columbia Pictures.

The Long Gray Line.

John Ford was directing.

Who wouldn't want to work for John Ford?

Ford, originally, wanted John Wayne for the part, but "The Duke," thankfully, wasn't available.

The Long Gray Line was a true story.

I played "Marty Maher".

He was an old-time West Point athletic instructor.

Maureen O'Hara…Donald Crisp…and Ward Bond were my co-stars.

We shot it at the West Point Academy during the summer when most of the cadets are gone.

The Long Gray Line was my first box-office hit in some time.

I was thinking I might even get an Oscar nomination…

But, that didn't happen.

Instead, I went to South Africa, and did *Untamed.*

It was my final film under my Fox contract.

I 'd been with them for eighteen years.

Fox did a lot for me, and I like to think the feeling is mutual.

Let's face it, though.

I've done an awful lot of stuff that's a monument to public patience.

I tried out a new play that closed before it hit Broadway…

And then, I did *The Eddy Duchin Story*.

Columbia shot it in Technicolor.

I just faked playing the piano.

Carmen Cavallero was the real talent behind the keyboard.

My co-star in *The Eddy Duchin Story* was Kim Novak.

I know she's big box-office these days, but…

Confusion between temperament and bad manner is unfortunate.

And, that's all I'm going to say on the subject.

———

Except that, *The Eddy Duchin Story* was a big hit.
(*Beat*)
After *Eddy Duchin*, I went back to the theatre.

Did George Bernard Shaw's *The Devil's Disciple* in Manchester, England…

And later, on the West End.

The critics were not kind to me.

One of them said: "*No Shaw play is a one-man play*".

While I was in England, Ted Richmond and I formed an independent production company:

Copa Productions.

We shot a film for Columbia: *Abandon Ship!*.

I was the executive officer on a luxury liner that blows up when it hits a derelict mine.

Most of the film takes place on a lifeboat.

The boat is overloaded…and I have to decide who gets thrown off.

It was, actually, based on a true story.

After a moment:

———

54

Darryl Zanuck had resigned as production head at
Fox in 1956.

He was producing independently, and he came to me
with a project that I couldn't turn down.

How can you turn down an Ernest Hemingway
project?

The picture was *The Sun Also Rises*.

It was about the "lost generation".

We were going to shoot in Spain…Paris… Mexico…

It had Ava Gardner… Errol Flynn… Mel Ferrer…
Eddie Albert…Me.

I'm told that Hemingway didn't like the picture.

They say he walked out after twenty-five minutes.
(Beat)
Initially, I turned down the tole of "Leonard Vole" in
Witness for the Prosecution.

I didn't feel my film career was going that well…

I wanted to work on the stage.

If you do a scene in a film…and it goes well…

The director says "*Cut and Print*," and it's over.

———

Your performance is there forever.

On stage, you get to do that good scene several times a week.

Billy Wilder didn't give up.

And, when he came to me with an offer of $300,000…

How could I turn him down?
(*Beat*)
After that, I hosted the "NBC Standard Oil Show" with Kay Thompson and Jimmy Durante.

Did a limited New York run of Shaw's *Back to Methuselah* with Faye Emerson.

That's when I met Deborah.

Deborah Montgomery Minarodos.

She was a friend of Linda Christian's brother-in-law.

Go figure.

One thing led to another…

In May, we married

I know…

She's twenty-six…and I'm forty-four.

But, it's love.

And, hopefully, we'll be having a son.

Life is good.

My marriage is good.

And now, I have to study my script.

George Sanders and I will be practicing our
swordplay later on.

Be sure to see *Solomon and Sheba* when it's released.

It should be a good one.

*He sits; picks up his script and
studies it, as* LIGHTS FADE.

ANNOUNNCER

On November 15, 1958, during the filming of the duel scene in *Solomon and Sheba*, Tyrone Power suffered a fatal heart attack.

He was forty-four years old..

In January of 1959, Deborah Power gave birth to a son.

He was named Tyrone William Power.

THE END

THE HOLLYWOOD LEGENDS is a series of one and two-person, two-act plays by Hollywood historian, screenwriter and playwright Michael B. Druxman that explore the life and times of some of filmdom's most glittering personalities.

From Clara Bow, "The 'It' Girl" of the silent era, through the birth of the talkies with Al Jolson and Maurice Chevalier, on through the thirties and forties with superstars like Clark Gable, Spencer Tracy, Carole Lombard, Errol Flynn, Basil Rathbone, Jeanette MacDonald and Nelson Eddy, Ida Lupino, Dick Powell, Clifton Webb, Yvonne De Carlo, Gary Cooper, Audrey Hepburn, Roy Scheider, Jason Robards, Larry Parks, Bud Abbott, Maureen O'Hara, Abe Vigoda, Christopher Lee, Ronald Reagan, Claire Trevor, Gale Sondergaard, Paul Muni, Mary Pickford, Jack Carter, Rod Steiger, Robert Preston, Gig Young, John Ireland, Esther Williams, and, finally, Hollywood's "boy genius," Orson Welles, these anecdote-filled dramatic pieces present a humorous, often touching portrait of each star and the era in which he/she lived.

The collection has now been expanded to include multiple character plays like: LANA & JOHNNY WERE LOVERS (Lana Turner), SEXY REXY (Rex Harrison). B MOVIE, which deals with the Franchot Tone/ Barbara Payton/Tom Neal scandal of the 1950s, ROBINSON & RAFT (Edward G. Robinson, George Raft), THE LAST MONSTERS (Bela Lugosi, Lon Chaney, Jr. & John Carradine), AVA & HER GUYS (Ava Gardner, Mickey Rooney, Artie Shaw, Frank Sinatra), BRODERICK CRAWFORD, and CLOWNS ON THE GROUND (Milton Berle, Joe E. Brown, Bert Lahr).

The plays, many of which have seen several productions, utilize simple costumes and props, and are designed to be staged on a single setting, with shifts in lighting to denote changes in time and place.

All questions with regard to licensing should be addressed to the author: Michael B. Druxman, PMB 119, 4301 W. William Cannon Dr., Suite B-150, Austin, TX 78749 [*druxy@ix.netcom.com*].